To Andrew [illegible]

Thanks for the
Training

From
Daniel Oke
2016

ANCIENT PRINCIPLES FOR SUCCESS

10 Keys to
Personal and
Business Triumph

Daniel Oke

authorHOUSE®

AuthorHouse™
1663 Liberty Drive
Bloomington, IN 47403
www.authorhouse.com
Phone: 1-800-839-8640

Unless otherwise indicated, all Scripture quotations are taken from the Holy Bible. New Living Translation, copyright © 1996, 2004, 2007 by Tyndale House Foundation. Used by permission of Tyndale House Publishers, Inc., Carol Stream, Illinois 60188. All rights reserved.

First published by AuthorHouse   01/28/2012

ISBN: 978-1-4678-8348-1 (sc)
ISBN: 978-1-4678-8349-8 (ebk)

Printed in the United States of America

Contents

About the Author

Daniel Oke is the co-founder of TeamEagle, a training organisation. He and his wife, Terri, created TeamEagle to train, mentor, and motivate his team to achieve personal success in the journey towards attaining their financial goals.

Daniel currently travels the UK as a trainer and motivational speaker. He has held several seminars and trainings with seasoned speakers like Bernie De Souza, best-selling author of *Your Success Is Hidden in Your Daily Routine*.

Daniel has no university degree, as he left formal education just before completing his sixth form; however, Daniel had the good fortune of growing up in a home where the pursuit of knowledge and love of learning thrived. His father cultivated in all his children a healthy desire to seek out the secrets hidden in books and to always subscribe to personal development. Daniel grew up surrounded by books and magazines—from *Reader's Digest* and *National Geographic*, to all sorts of manuals, books, and encyclopaedias. To say the least, Daniel developed his interest in personal development early in life and has kept that interest alive and well throughout his life. This has allowed him access to a greater wealth of knowledge than he could never have acquired in any subjective or formal educational system. Daniel is truly living proof that success in life isn't exclusively dependent on achieving academic accomplishment.

Daniel is also a pastor and teacher who has taught biblical principles for twenty-five years. The success principles explored in *The Ancient Principles for Success* are age-old fundamental truths that he has lived and relied upon himself. Relying upon these principles has created otherwise unimaginable lifestyles and success for many around the world today—and it can do the same for you. Daniel retired from the civil service at the young age of forty-five. He and his family currently live in Milton Keynes, UK.

Dedication

**To my dad,
Domingo Michael Tunji Oke
1917-1975**

Royal Air Force—Second World War

**You were my first mentor; you inspired me to
expand my horizons. It was you who
first taught me about the value of curiosity
and also about seeking out the secrets
hidden in books.**

Special Dedication

To my wife, Terri, for being a partner, a supporter, and a solid foundation on whom I can always depend when it counts.

And to my kids—Daniel, Charis, and Sophia—for being my inspiration and the reason I never give up keeping the dream alive.

Foreword

When I first met Daniel Oke, I knew that success and personal development were on his mind. He was extremely focused on what he wanted, and he was well equipped to successfully get it. One year on, and Daniel has managed to stay on the same path, bring his goals to fruition, and pass on his knowledge to others.

Daniel is definitely a friend and an influence I shall always treasure, and I'm quite delighted and privileged to contribute towards the success and goal of this work—even if only by writing these few lines. I am happy and excited about the impact this book will have on you, as of course it has already had on me. Daniel has shone a light into the mindset of the ancients, and in doing so has revealed an all-but-forgotten treasure trove of knowledge. I share Daniel's belief that this treasure trove can ultimately revolutionise the attitude we have towards business and financial security, and I applaud his decision to share his discovery with the world by writing this book.

Ancient Principles of Success walks you through ten principles that teach us what we need to do in order to live our dreams. It shows that truths are never lost, just forgotten; it proves that ideas are never too old that they cannot be beneficial in our current age. Many discoveries today have their roots in ancient mathematics and scientific theories. It is thanks to the existence of ancient records that modern man is able to understand and control his environment to the extent that he does today. *Ancient Principles of Success* will also help you understand another environment—the environment of business and success—and it will help you control this environment to whatever extent you want, just as it has helped me.

This book has shown me that the relevance of ancient knowledge is not limited to the field of science, nor should it be. Only recently

I had a conversation with a friend, and we discussed how ancient history created and taught us what we know today! All the successful people in today's day and age have followed a certain tip or belief that was shaped by history, and Daniel presents that very well in this book.

If, like me, you are interested in self-development or have a goal that you wish to accomplish, I suggest you read further. I hope that you enjoy this book as much as I have, and that you put what you have learned into action.

Hanieh Chehrehnegari
Founder, SpeakersKey

Acknowledgements

This project would never have been possible much less realised without the help and support of various people in my life. I would now like to acknowledge and recognise these remarkable people without whom I would have had a less worthwhile experience.

Firstly, I would like to acknowledge both the late Pastor Colonel R. B. Thieme Jr of the Berachah Church in Dallas, Texas, and Pastor Bob McLaughlin of Grace Bible Church in Somerset, Massachusetts, for their spiritual guidance and grounding. You didn't know it, but the work you were doing had a profound impact in shaping a life 5,000 miles away.

I will forever be indebted to you, Jaz Hanspal, my first business mentor and an excellent leader. You helped create in me the discipline of leadership and the understanding that in order to help yourself, you must first help others. Your guidance stretched and challenged me, but in the long run it built my business backbone, together with the IBS (International Business System) training and business mentoring programme.

To Hanieh Chehrehnegari and Bernie De Souza, I ask, "How can I thank you enough?" Though I'm at loss to express my appreciation in mere words, I shall simply say thanks a million for your advice and constructive feedback, and for taking the time to read the raw manuscript. Hanieh, I thank you for writing the foreword. Bernie, I thank you for writing the blurb on the back page.

I would also like to express my gratitude to Modupe Shonubi and Mark Delicate. Mark, you were a total stranger to me until the crucial moment needed. It goes to show that there is truth in the words of John Burroughs: "Leap and a net will appear." I hardly knew you, but you chose to trust me, regardless; you were instrumental in opening doors for funding when things were looking a little bleak for the project. Thank you! Modupe thanks for being the human equivalent of a Swiss army knife, indubitably you are a true life saver. Your friendship over the years has been precious to me and valued thank you.

Thanks, everyone, for all you have done and for your trust: you were all strategic in making everything come together in exactly the right time.

I have saved my greatest gratitude for last. To my Lord and Saviour, Jesus Christ be all the glory, for it is in Him and by Him that all things are made possible.

Introduction

Earl Nightingale is probably one of the world's most respected and recognised motivational speakers and personal development experts. In 1956 he produced what is arguably the world's most celebrated recording—a veritable benchmark of excellence in motivational speaking—*The Strangest Secret*. This one recording produced decades before its time is still very much relevant today, as those who seek excellence would no doubt agree. It has sold over a million copies worldwide, and it focuses on one simple theme: you are what you think. A quote from the recording advises, "Here's the key to success and the key to failure: we become what we think about." Half a century earlier, in 1903, a British poet and philosopher, James Allen, also produced one of the most inspirational writings of all time, *As a Man Thinketh*, based on the biblical proverb "As a man thinketh in his heart so is he." Allen's publication became a global runaway success, valued as canon in its own right amongst entrepreneurs and business owners, and adopted and used by corporate organisations. In more recent times a new revolution in understanding and harnessing the power of personal development took the world by storm. In 2007 Rhonda Byrne published her accomplished work, *The Secret*. The book alone globally sold more than four million copies and the DVD more than two million. Here again we see the influence of the Bible, as the central theme of this magnificent work is the Law of Attraction: "what you think about you bring about," or "thoughts become things."

Since ancient times and straight through to the modern age, those who have understood the value and effectiveness of ancient wisdom have continued to keep it alive today. Champions of ancient wisdom exist amongst authors, mentors, and motivational speakers, such as John Maxwell, Zig Ziglar, Denis Waitley, Brian Tracy, and of course the late Jim Rohn—all very successful and highly sought-after trainers, motivational speakers, and writers. All these individuals focus their attention on the current corporate and business world, and all are fervent advocates of the ancient principles still so easily accessible today.

The value of ancient wisdom is so blatantly apparent that it would be utter stupidity to ignore it. The structure of business may have changed over the centuries—which is expected, as technology is the driving force behind trends today, where information technology and automated technology (robotics) drive manufacturing and production industries. Developments in aviation in just a few short decades has seen more and more products and services delivered downline in record time; however, behind the veil of technology is the soul of the revolution in business today—and that is people. Business can be impersonal, but people cannot be, and the success or failure of any business depends on the mental attitude of its people, and even more so, its founders. All this confirms the need to value and utilise ancient wisdom.

Evidence has shown that over the past 150 years the greatest minds have had a strong respect for the Bible as a source of unparalleled wisdom—far too valuable to ignore. Furthermore, many successful business owners today will admit to either using biblical principles as a direct source, or at least indirectly through books, publications, or attending motivational seminars in which the speaker has used these principles to drive their message of success. Ignore it at your own business peril! I believe I am just giving credit where it's due.

So, you may ask, why have I written the book? Well, it is not my intension to take a spiritual stand of any kind. This is not because many might get turned off by that but merely to draw attention to the simple fact that many of these principles are laws of divine establishment which preclude any specific religious belief system; they are simply laws that will work regardless of who or what you believe in. *He causes his sun to rise on the evil and the good, and sends rain on the righteous and the unrighteous.* [Matthew 5:45]

The principle of guaranteed return repeats the words of the Bible: *Whatsoever a man sows so shall he reap.* A man is a man is a man, not culture or creed or belief system; you will reap what you sow, plain and simple. Anyone can utilise these principles because that is what they are there for. The truth is, many have already accomplished this, and more will continue to do so. Business may have changed, but the principles of success haven't—we have just forgotten them. Sometimes we think there is something better than these ancient truths, but there isn't. Even all the new ideas are still rooted deeply in the ancient principles; you just have to know where to find them. *What has been will be again, what has been done will be done again; there is nothing new under the sun.* [Ecclesiastes 1:9]

I have written this book simply to reset the sextant and get back on course by understanding the mindset of those who started it all thousands of years ago. There is nothing new under the sun; it's all been done before, so shouldn't we then get back to the beginning—or at least as close as possible? Shouldn't we get back to the basics of success principles?

[**AUTHOR'S NOTE:** *Throughout, biblical quotations are set in italics, with parts that I wish to emphasise set in bold and italics. Quotations from other sources are set in plain type, surrounded by quotation marks. Other points that I wish to emphasise are set in bold.*]

Above all, I give thanks.

Now to Him who is able to do immeasurably more than all we ask or imagine, according to His power that is at work within us, to Him be the glory.

Chapter 1

THE PRINCIPLE

Guaranteed Returns

> **Genesis 8:22** (New International Version)
> *As long as the earth endures, seedtime and harvest,*
> *cold and heat, summer and winter, day and night will*
> *never cease.*

Most people simply live their lives generally oblivious to the well-balanced and acutely tuned mechanism that governs the universe. Whether we are aware of this or not, however, the universe holds us all inextricably in its grip, and we must obey its laws. Unless we begin to learn and understand the laws that govern the machine, any hope of maintaining an autonomous and fruitful life will be impossible.

The principle of guaranteed returns is one of the oldest laws of the ancients. God proclaimed this law for the very first time in the verse above from the book of Genesis.

Certain natural laws that command gain and loss govern us and our lives, whether we accept it or not. Many of us are either oblivious to this fact or have resigned ourselves to believe that we cannot consciously effect a change, and therefore we must leave things as they are. Whilst a small minority has chosen to study these laws and adopt them, which allows them to naturally create a bubble or environment filled with positive returns in their lives.

3

Activating the Law of Guaranteed Returns

Seedtime and harvest, cold and heat, summer and winter, day and night . . . as you can see, there is an obvious pattern that isn't alien to science, contemporary beliefs, the natural order of things, or any other laws at that. This is a well-balanced principle, it is a dance, it is the law of "give and receive". Newton discovered this law several thousand years after it was written in the Bible. In his theory of motion he said, "To every action there is **always** an equal and opposite reaction."

The universe will carry on doing its thing, and you will have to choose to do one of three things: get out of its way, get crushed, or work with it. Only one of these options is productive. The farmer is of the seasons, and whether he wills it or not, these seasons are immovable. They are a force of nature, and they will come about and complete their cycles. There isn't much the farmer can do about it save to be prepared and work with it in order to reap a bountiful harvest.

Many people prepare for these seasons in their own ways. For example, in winter you might choose to insulate your home or buy a new winter coat; in spring maybe buy an umbrella or raincoat; in summer you break out the holiday brochure or buy a new pair of sunglasses; in autumn you have a rake at the ready. Regardless of your preparations, the seasons will come as they must.

The farmer chooses to activate the inherent untapped possibilities of abundance hidden within the seasons—an abundance governed by law that guarantees an unchangeable process. **Seedtime and harvest shall not cease.** He understands that he has a choice and a role to play, and he chooses wisely to play that role.

Abundance and increase are within our grasp, but many of us can't see it. Postmodern myopia has effectively blinded us, leaving us unable to see beyond the veil of modernism, and thus we find it difficult to perceive the wisdom of the ancients.

The Harvest Is Abundance

You will reap what you sow. We are all inextricably woven into this principle; hence whatever you sow, you will reap the same **in abundance.** If you sow nothing, you will reap nothing (the same in abundance). There is no abstention from this law, so you may as well participate—and do so positively. Many come across fantastic opportunities daily that have been brought along their paths, and yet they choose to do nothing in response. They will then wonder why things aren't going well, and why they have no money and more debt. As I said, the law is constantly at work, and you cannot just choose to abstain. If you sow nothing, you will reap nothing—literally, a great big zero and in abundance.

You must learn to trust the principles. They say success leaves clues. If you ask most successful entrepreneurs today, you will find that they too learned these principles; but above all, they work with these principles like the farmer does. Those who succeed sow their seeds and then wait for the season to reap their abundant harvests. Now you too must learn to trust in the principle of guaranteed returns. Commit your precious seeds to the fields and wait for the time to harvest your bountiful crop.

Chapter 2

THE PRINCIPLE

Risk Pays Dividend; Safety Leads to Ruin

Matthew 25:14-29 (New Living Translation)
. . . the story of a man going on a long trip. He called together his servants and entrusted his money to them while he was gone. He gave five bags of silver to one, two bags of silver to another, and one bag of silver to the last—dividing it in proportion to their abilities. He then left on his trip.

The servant who received the five bags of silver began to invest the money and earned five more. The servant with two bags of silver also went to work and earned two more. But the servant who received the one bag of silver dug a hole in the ground and hid the master's money.

After a long time their master returned from his trip and called them to give an account of how they had used his money. The servant to whom he had entrusted the five bags of silver came forward with five more and said, "Master, you gave me five bags of silver to invest, and I have earned five more."

The master was full of praise. "Well done, my good and faithful servant. You have been faithful in handling this small amount, so now I will give you many more responsibilities. Let's celebrate together!"

9

The servant who had received the two bags of silver came forward and said, "Master, you gave me two bags of silver to invest, and I have earned two more."

The master said, "Well done, my good and faithful servant. You have been faithful in handling this small amount, so now I will give you many more responsibilities. Let's celebrate together!"
Then the servant with the one bag of silver came and said, "Master, I knew you were a harsh man, harvesting crops you didn't plant and gathering crops you didn't cultivate. I was afraid I would lose your money, so I hid it in the earth. Look, here is your money back."

But the master replied, "You wicked and lazy servant! If you knew I harvested crops I didn't plant and gathered crops I didn't cultivate, why didn't you deposit my money in the bank? At least I could have gotten some interest on it."

Then he ordered, "Take the money from this servant, and give it to the one with the ten bags of silver. To those who use well what they are given, even more will be given, and they will have an abundance. But from those who do nothing, even what little they have will be taken away."

Why the Poor Get Poorer and the Rich Get Richer

If you stand still long enough, it is almost certain that you will soon hear someone ask that old and prevalent question, why do the rich get richer and the poor get poorer?

For many, many years mankind has pondered this question, but the answer has been quite elusive; so much so that it has left us quite perplexed. Nevertheless, the answer to this centuries-old question has stared us in the face for thousands of years. Many people have come across the answer but have failed to recognise it or to connect its relevance in the modern era. It's almost as if there have been scales over our eyes that have prevented us from seeing truth. It is kind of like a blind spot: we see everything else quite clearly, but that which really matters remains invisible.

The answer to this big question is really quite simple, and it is the basis of the second principle.

The parable of the talents tells the story of a master (in today's terms a mentor) going on a journey and leaving his servants (mentees) with various amounts of money, each entrusted with an amount that he should be able to handle. Some of the translations of this parable use the word *talent*, which was simply a unit of currency used in that period. Calculations have estimated that the servants would have had \$5,000.00, \$2,000.00, and \$1,000.00, respectively, in today's currency.

We then learned that two of the mentees actually invested the money that had been given to them, but one did not. Out of fear, he buried the money: *I was afraid I would lose your money, so I hid it in the earth.* Shall we investigate the consequences of this particular ill-advised decision? To some it might seem a bit harsh on the part of the mentor to punish the mentee in the way that he did, but please do not forget that this was just a parable meant to teach us an essential lesson: by way of our own weak decisions and **fears,** we frequently bring the worst upon ourselves financially and otherwise.

The Mentor's Judgement

Then he ordered, "Take the money from this servant, and give it to the one with the ten bags of silver. To those who use well what they are given, even more will be given, and they will have an abundance. But from those who do nothing, even what little they have will be taken away."

We live in a world today where opportunities are abundant; in addition, we have access to tons of books and reference materials dedicated to learning how to harness these opportunities. If you are

11

willing to tap into this wisdom, you can create unbelievable wealth for yourself. Yet many would rather just carry on like remote-controlled automatons, going from home to work, work to home, every day, year in and year out. They complain about the job every day of the week. Every Friday they're off to the pub with a refreshing feeling of "TGIF! Work is over for a couple of days." But then all they talk about the entire evening is work. And yet, we ask why the rich people are getting richer!

How do I know all this? Well, that used to be me as well.

We go to work, come back home, and at the end of the week or month we get paid our wages. But how many people think at that moment, "OK, here is some money. I should invest it to make more." We live in fear and make decisions out of fear. We think, what if I lose everything? So the fear of loss forces us to make poor decisions based on poor judgment. What are the consequences of making decisions like this? After they receive their wages—or talents, to follow the parable—most people spend the money! They pay their bills, which is necessary, as you don't want to be in debt, but most spending is about gratification rather than investing. Here are some examples: two or three mobile phones, cable TV, new car, holiday, shopping, pub, eating out, etc. Well let's look closely at these trends to see what is really going on.

The big question is, who controls all the companies and services that we all so easily spend our hard-earned cash on every month? In the UK, SKY is owned by Rupert Murdoch; 2010 revenue for BSkyB was £5.9 billion, up 10 per cent. Cable TV in the UK is controlled, at least for now, by Virgin Media, owned by Richard Branson. Virgin Media's 2008 revenue was £10.16 billion. BMW founder Franz Josef Popp; 2010 profit £2.81 billion. Thomas Cook Group PLC, leading provider of leisure travel and holidays in the UK; Chairman Michael Beckett, net income £22.8 million; Tesco PLC, the UK shopping giant; founder Jack Cohen, 2010 revenue £62.54 billion. Now do you clearly see the pattern?

We all earn money—hard cash every month, our "talents"—but how many people think beyond spending? How many think about doing something more productive with their money like investing it? When we spend it we don't realise that the rich are like the wise servants/mentees in the parable of the talents: they have learned how to invest the little they originally had, and now they have gained more. However, they get even more than imagined because everyone else who refuses to invest surrenders their portion too—that is, the little they have is taken from them and given to those who already have more. In current terms the poor give the little they have to the rich as a result of mindless consumerism. This is the reason why the rich get richer and the poor get poorer.

Risk pays dividends, and safety leads to ruin. Running away from the responsibility to yourself and your financial future is a big mistake; you cannot just bury your head in the sand thinking that if you can't see the problem it doesn't exist. The shocker is that the problem is still there, and there is probably going to be a serious consequence for burying your head in the sand in the first place: *even what little they have will be taken away.* Rather than taking on the challenge and gunning for it, there are ways and solutions to achieve effective results. As I pointed out earlier on in this chapter, if you are willing to learn and maintain an open mind you can change everything around you. Read books, attend seminars, and listen to audios that espouse these ancient principles, and you will start creating the mindset that will make you a better person and a fearless entrepreneur.

Chapter 3

THE PRINCIPLE

Fear Leads to Decrease;
Belief Leads to Increase

> **Matthew 14:29** (New Living Translation)
> *So Peter went over the side of the boat and walked on the water toward Jesus. But when he saw the strong wind and the waves, he was terrified and began to sink. "Save me, Lord!" he shouted.*

We make decisions based mostly on emotion. Our emotions play a major role in how we handle various situations in our lives, as well as in the way in which we respond to pressure. However, emotion is just one side of a two-sided coin; the other side of the coin contains our logic. Logic helps us stay grounded and focused; therefore, relying solely on our emotions would be akin to setting sail without a map. The trouble is that over the last few hundred years there has been a steady decline in people's concern with building strong emotional foundations. Ask people seventy years of age or older, and they will tell you stories of what life was like for them growing up. They'll also tell you the stories that their parents and grandparents told them about when they grew up and had to endure even more than their children did. Above all, they would tell you how grateful they are for living during those times, because they still draw on the wisdom of the lessons learned and strengths built as a result of growing up in that era. Many of them will express their frustration over the decline in the current age, of basic principles like character and courage. Let's face it: the world isn't what it used to be, period. In the past we looked up to certain individuals as our source of inspirational leadership—or at least our parents and grandparents did—Sir Winston Churchill, Abraham Lincoln, Mahatma Gandhi. John F. Kennedy, Dr Martin Luther King Jr, etc.

As you can see, many great leaders have existed over time, but our present time has witnessed a steady decline in leadership. In this present generation few exhibit the traits essential to emerging in roles of leadership, much less great leadership. Society evolves constantly, socially as well as culturally, and what it deemed necessary a hundred years ago it now regards as out of date. Today's current wave of evolution seems to strip all traces of the foundation from which true leadership and emotional stability have developed for centuries. An interest in history has been replaced with daytime TV talk shows and the pop idol culture; reading books has been replaced with the games console, social media, and Internet surfing.

In this current wave of emotional evolution, our present generation is inherently more prone to seeking entertainment or self-gratification rather than to cultivating character. In fact, I would be so bold as to add that, given what I had to live through growing up in Africa—or what my father and grandfather had taught me about their own lives growing up—and what I know for certain about my kids today who have never been to Africa, today's younger generation would definitely find it hard to muster the emotional strength it will take to live as prior generations have done. So why is this relevant to the principle? As I said earlier, we all make decisions based mostly on emotion, but logic also plays a part in the decision-making process. Logic has its roots in our frame of reference—that is, what we've learned from our past but not necessarily what we have actually experienced. We can benefit from what we have learned by reading or understanding the lessons of history. George Santayana puts it better: "Those who cannot learn from history are doomed to repeat it." Of course, we also draw from our environment, associations, allegiances, cultural influences, etc.

So, if we take a closer look at our society today, we will see a society working hard to extricate itself from its strong stable roots, its anchor.

As our society becomes more sophisticated, any thought process deemed not current is simply uprooted and thrown out. Sadly, this has included the Bible, one of the world's most reliable sources of ancient wisdom. We now live in a society in which 95 per cent are largely clones of one another. You will find that, regardless of the geographical reference point, people are generally the same—they listen to the same music, watch the same TV, worship the same pop idols, dress the same, and speak the same social media language. Thus, they largely think the same and make the same choices. Consequently, in a society that lacks a strong frame of reference, most people will make choices influenced by fear.

The Decision-Making Matrix

As I mentioned before, we mostly make decisions based on our emotions, but it helps to have a sound grounding in logic. Our logic acts as an anchor, helping to prevent our emotions from running riot. Logic also serves as a frame of reference (position or orientation), allowing us to recall/retrieve events or information from the past. This will ensure that we make most of our decisions from a position of strength rather than weakness.

Many people have been put in their place, so to speak, by their environment; they have lived most of their lives reminded that they are losers. Such reminders come from varied sources—their so-called friends, their teachers, bosses, creditors, bank managers, etc.—but they result in the same attitude of defeat. Most people have become akin to cowering animals, with their tails tucked between their legs, and have totally beaten down egos. Therefore, when most face the crucial opportunity to make a life-changing decision, they panic. In that moment when they look to their experiences or frame of reference for inspiration and courage, they see only fear, doubt, doom, and gloom, and so they shrink away. They have no strengths to draw on. Consequently, they constantly make their decisions from a position of weakness, which inevitably leads to failure.

19

The Failure Matrix

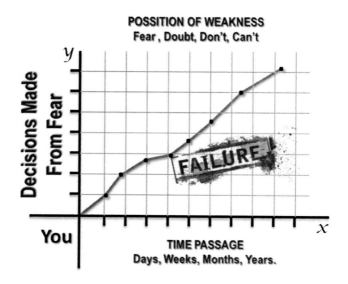

POSSITION OF WEAKNESS
Fear, Doubt, Don't, Can't

Decisions made out of fear demonstrate weakness. Fear is designed to keep you in the status quo, frozen in time and lacking forward momentum. Instead of progress and success, decline, degeneration, and/or financial and spiritual downturns result. Failure does not occur overnight but in small increments over time. You are today a sum total of the decisions you have made over the passage of time; if fear and doubt have ruled your decisions, you have made those decisions from a position of weakness—regardless of whether you realised it at the time.

Each dot inside the grid in the failure matrix (figure above) represents every decision made in fear and doubt, based on such thoughts as "I can't"; "I'm not sure it's for me"; "I'm not good at doing that"; "I have too much on my plate"; "My husband/wife won't let me"; "I can't afford it"; and so forth. You know these excuses; that's why they sound so familiar. In addition to the dots representing those fear-based decisions, the failure matrix shows time (x-axis), measured in days, weeks, months, or years. Hence, we can see that failure occurs in increments. Every time we make the wrong choice, we bolster our future in possible ruin; time and history determine the final outcome.

However, all is not lost, because we can always choose to change! We can do a 180-degree turnaround anytime we want.

The road to success is similar to the road to failure, in that the mechanisms are the same, but the power base is different. Success draws energy from faith and belief. Another important ingredient in success is frame of reference, which allows you to draw your experiences from a positive source. Frame of reference is particularly important, and there are many ways to draw on it. Books about success principles allow you to draw from the written wisdom of other people. Coaches and mentors allow you to draw on the wisdom and personal expertise of those who seek to help you. Friends and associations allow you to draw from peer groups with the same aims and objectives. History allows you to draw from past lessons, helping you to avoid repeating disasters. Combine all these together as your frame of reference, and your journey to success has begun, headed in the right direction.

Success Matrix

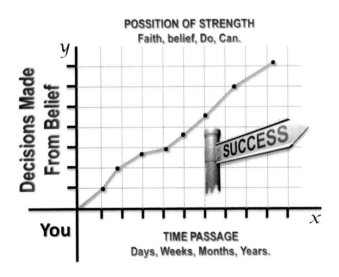

Apart from the above-captioned differences, everything else in the success matrix works the same as the failure matrix. Sometimes we are so close to totally transforming our lives that we have no

21

idea just how close we really are. The journey to success is simply deciding to stay committed to making a series of decisions from a position of strength; over time you will arrive at your desired destination—whatsoever that may be—through one positive decision at a time. Altering your "self-talk" from the negative to the positive with statements like "Yes, I can"; "I will"; "I'm capable"; "I will find a way"; "I will overcome it"; "It won't be a problem"; and so on, will foster an optimistic mindset. Positive self-talk will begin to force your mind to seek solutions; it will activate innate tools within the mind specially dedicated to solving problems. Let's call this the problem-solving tool (PST) of the mind. Those who shrink away from possibilities never develop these skills or tools, and so their minds have no experience or frame of reference for managing challenges or solving problems. They usually give in before the opportunity to think of a solution even presents itself. Their favourite words are "I can't"; once they give in to that mentality, no reason to seek further possibilities exists, and their minds shut down. They never engage PST, so their lives carry on in status quo indefinitely! They don't participate in the race, so how can they ever win?

A while ago I came across an interview which Will Smith did with Charlie Rose, talking about building a wall. Here is what Will Smith said: "You don't set out to build a wall. You don't say 'I'm going to build the biggest, baddest, greatest wall that's ever been built.' You don't start there. You say, 'I'm going to lay this brick as perfectly as a brick can be laid.' You do that every single day. And soon you have a wall."

So you can, and will, become successful once you've realised that all it takes is consistently making a series of decisions from a position of strength, which eventually creates your success.

The Lesson in Peter's Story

Back to the Bible lesson that opened this chapter. There are two parts to the lesson of Peter's story. The first part deals with Peter's belief and frame of reference. Peter knew who Jesus was; he was well aware of what Jesus was capable of because of His reputation, as well as Peter's own observation that Jesus was actually approaching the boat Himself, walking on water. Jesus was their mentor, and they had access to His personal experiences and expertise—this is one of the crucial resources needed in building a solid frame of reference. The mentor teaches you not to fear; for if they can do it, you certainly can too. The second part deals with Peter's rejection of faith, causing him to demonstrate poor judgment. When Peter made his next decision from a position of weakness he immediately began to sink. The passage sheds light on the reason behind Peter's catastrophic judgment: *when he saw the strong wind and the waves,* **he was terrified** *and began to sink.* Peter simply took his eyes off his source of inspiration—the power source of his success—and focused it instead on his immediate 'reality'. As a result, he thought to himself something like, "This is insane: there is no way walking on water is possible!" Now with all that going on in his mind, he became terrified and began to feel the mighty rushing wind and the spray of the waves. His mental attitude finally descended into a catastrophic failure, and he began to sink (fell into ruins).

Chapter 4

THE PRINCIPLE

The Minority Rule
over the Majority

Matthew 22:14 (New Living Translation)
For many are called but few are chosen.

I remember the day I emailed my resignation to my manager at the JobCentre, where I had worked for about nine years. Within ten minutes of my sending the email, she rushed into my office and made a beeline for my desk, clutching a printed copy of my email in her hands and looking rather shocked. I could clearly discern the stress in her voice as she said, "Are you sure about this? What are you going to do now? How are you going to pay your bills?" What about this and what about that? Her frantic questions went on and on.

I suppose these are all valid fears or concerns, which many of us have to face on a daily basis. In fact, these are the thoughts that occupy most people's waking hours; they are also the reason why many people are too scared to do anything about them. My manager felt she had to remind me that the decision I had just made could potentially—or even inevitably—lead to my ruin. In her eyes, she was looking out for me. It does not matter if you live in the richest or the poorest country in the world: if you do the same as the people around you, you will have a 95 per cent chance of failure. Statistics and studies have shown that only 5 per cent will make life-changing decisions that will lead them to become wealthy or financially secure; 95 per cent will do what everyone else does. Other major writers and experts around the world have treated this same fact extensively (please refer to the list of recommended reading and audio). It is good to know that the majority is usually wrong! Only a minority will believe in themselves enough to take action; only a minority will desire to walk the lonely path to success and face the consequences of ridicule and rejection. This minority is the 5 per cent. Most people will say, "If it's that easy, why isn't everyone doing it?" The majority is the 95 per cent.

Now having said all that, let me clarify that this does not necessarily mean that the rest of the population is doomed to failure. The principle actually starts off with a positive: *Many are called*. This means that everyone has the inner potential to become great. To better understand this principle, we need to look further back in history. Let's examine the origin of the word potential. Middle English "potencial", from Late Latin "potentialis", from "potentia"; "potentiality", from Latin, "power", from "potent-" "potens"; first known use: fourteenth century (*Merriam-Webster*).

Two other words to note in the paragraph above are the words **power** and **potent.** We all have the power within us to become whatever we choose to become—failures or winners—**potential** simply means that we can choose. A stick of dynamite has the potential to level a man's house, but someone has to light the fuse. Now let's look at the application of the word **potential:**

1. Possible, as opposed to actual existing in possibility: capable of development into actuality capable of being or becoming.
2. Possibility; potentiality; a latent excellence or ability that may or may not be developed.

So why is it that so few people actually realise their own potential? I mean, if we have all been called, why are only a few chosen? Therein lies the answer: "choice". Few choose to change the outcomes in their lives; most choose not to. The second and final part of this is built on the principle of choice. The problem is not so much that few are physically chosen and made to succeed against their will, but more so that many have chosen **not** to succeed; hence, they are subsequently rejected by the principle of choice.

This is very much like the self-fulfilling prophecy: A man tells himself, and sometimes people around him, that he is a good-for-nothing; he considers himself a failure. He spends most of his waking hours entertaining this thought process and thereby strengthening it; then he haphazardly takes on life challenges, expecting to fail, which, of course, he does. He gets the exact results he expected from the choice he has made, and his attitude of **failure** comes as expected. This man would often defend his never-ending failure by affirming it to himself and everyone around him: "Did I not say it? Did I not tell you I couldn't do that? I've always known that with my luck it was all going to go wrong."

The principle of choice is a double-edged blade: it actually swings and cuts both ways. If you choose to be brave and make quality decisions and quality choices, the universe responds and in turn chooses you right back. It's so blatantly plain to see. The majority (95 per cent) have a very low level of expectation in life; they move from one place to the other, with their shoulders hunched and their chins tucked in defeat. They have rejected possibilities, and so possibilities have rejected them right back. They have embraced mediocrity, and so mediocrity has embraced them right back. The next thing they do is flock; finding people like themselves to swap ideas and advice with, but they never do anything that will greatly affect or change their lives. Sometimes they find someone ready to make the right choices and start the process of becoming great, in which case they descend on the poor fellow with a barrage of questions: Are you sure about this? What are you going to do now? How are you going to pay your bills? What about this and what about that? Much as my well-meaning manager did.

The ancients have known about this principle since the dawn of time. Success is not a democracy where the majority carries the vote. Just because statistics show that there are more poor people than rich does not mean that you cannot be rich! As a matter of fact, the principle works in reverse—i.e., the fact that a few have been successful means that you *can*. This principle is also known as "If you can do it, so can I."

In American history there was never a black president till President Barack Obama. This is not because there has never been a black candidate running for office; in fact, five black candidates have run for the US presidency:

Shirley Chisholm (30 November 1924-1 January 2005). Congresswoman representing New York's 12th Congressional District, she was the first black woman elected to Congress. On 25 January 1972, she became the first major-party black candidate for President of the United States and the first woman to run for the Democratic presidential nomination.

Rev Jesse Jackson, Sr (8 October 1941—). Black American civil rights activist and Baptist minister. November 1983 through 1984 mounted his campaign for US presidency; he was the second African American to campaign for the presidency (Shirley Chisholm was the first).

Carol Braun (16 August 1947—) Represented the state of Illinois in the United States Senate from 1993 to 1999. First—and for now only—black woman elected to the United States Senate, she was a candidate for the Democratic presidential nomination during the 2004 campaign.

Rev Al Sharpton, Jr (3 October 1954—) American Baptist minister, also a civil rights activist (like Jesse Jackson). In 2004 he was a candidate for the Democratic presidential nomination.

We all know the story of Barack Obama's election in 2008. He was one African American who refused to go by the past history of failure by black Americans, standing on the single-minded belief captured in his slogan, "Yes, we can!" Recognising the potential within himself, he made a decision. He chose to be the one who will make the difference; he chose success, and success chose him right back.

Socially and economically, much like the fingers on your hands, the world is not balanced. And there is nothing anyone can do about that. If you have been following current affairs you will be aware of the poor souls occupying major cities' financial districts, demanding that the world be made equal. But the truth is, nobody really wants to be equal to the next person. We live in a competitive world, and that competition creates growth and excellence. Without growth there is only death; this is simply natural. When a tree falls in the rain forest, the undergrowth immediately starts to compete for the space that has been created. In a very short time the opportunity to get some sunlight is closed till another tree falls. If you are not healthy enough to compete, you have to be satisfied with others treading upon you. Please do not hate me! I did not make the rules; governments can legislate, but they cannot change the natural order of things. We have all seen the failure of the Eastern bloc's experiment with communism and its subsequent collapse.

Within our society today, experts put the figure for the rich and well off at 5 per cent. The rest—the 95 per cent—are just getting by in some shape or another. For many, their future financial plan involves wining a lottery jackpot. That is not much of a plan. The minority (5 per cent of the population) holds 95 per cent of all global wealth, but every one of us has the potential to be a part of the well-off minority. I suppose if that happened it wouldn't be a minority anymore; but then again, only 5 per cent of the population will actually make the choice necessary to achieve financial independence.

Will you be one of the 5 per cent?

Chapter 5

THE PRINCIPLE

Enterprise over Slavery

Genesis 30:27-34 (Contemporary English Version)
*But Laban told him, "If you really are my friend, stay
on, and I'll pay whatever you ask. I'm sure the LORD
has blessed me because of you." Jacob answered:
"You've seen how hard I've worked for you, and you
know how your flocks and herds have grown under
my care. You didn't have much before I came, but the
LORD has blessed everything I have ever done for
you.* **Now it's time for me to start looking out
for my own family.** *How much do you want me
to pay you?" Laban asked. Then Jacob told him:* **"I
don't want you to pay me anything. Just do one
thing, and I'll take care of your sheep and goats. Let
me go through your flocks and herds and take
the sheep and goats that are either spotted or
speckled and the black lambs. That's all you
need to give me."**

There are three ways to earn an income on this planet today at
least—that is, there are three *legal* ways to earn an income—these
are linear income, leveraged income, and residual income (also called
passive income). From about the time of the onset of the Industrial
Revolution, most people were able to rely on income from labour
for the first time in history; later this labour became what we now
call careers or jobs. The Industrial Revolution created opportunities
for men, women, and even children to earn a living. However in the

midst of all the seeming prosperity, a trade-off arose: more and more people departed from the spirit of enterprise in favour of "having a job". The more people embraced this mentality, the more they drifted away from embracing the business enterprise and their own success and financial independence.

The Linear Income

We all make our incomes in diverse ways within the global economy. However, regardless of the system or method specifically utilised by each person, the reason for generating income remains the same: to attain economic and social balance. I like to refer to this process as the income-generating system (IGS).

Stage one of the IGS is the linear income, which is the type of income that most people favour and which includes employment, self-employment, and retail. We can recognise this type of income by its primary building block: Time. Without time it is practically impossible to create linear income. To clarify, time plays a role in all other types of income, but with linear income, it's the *only* way to create income, as opposed to leveraged or residual (passive) income, both of which only relatively involve time.

Time is linear and predictable, just like a clock. If you start your day at 8.00 a.m., you can take a lunch break from 12.00 p.m. to 1.00 p.m., leave at 5.00 p.m., and then do it all over again the following day, and the day after that, and so on. All this is true because time is linear and predictable. This is the reason why so many people prefer a job: they feel that it's predictable. I have lost count of how many conversations I have had with people who say, "Yeah, well, at least with a job I know just what I'm getting, and I also like the security." In truth, linear income is no more secure than a prison made of bamboo: the problem is that, unless you point out the flaws, most people won't bother looking for them. They'd rather just pretend that everything is OK, and most of them still are literally oblivious to the reality.

During the Industrial Revolution (approximately 1760-1860) it was common for people to expect to find a job and keep it for life.

The demand for labour in every industry on an almost global scale experienced a boom fanned by an endless supply of human labour quite akin to slavery. This created the working class, with an average wage for female factory workers set at seven shillings per week and for males at twenty to thirty shillings per week. Because of this very low income, many children had to go to work in factories as well. Thus, entire families went to work just to bolster their household income, and schooling and education became of little importance. For many, school was a luxury that they simply could not afford. Ultimately, though, the lack of education created an unforeseen secondary problem. The working class, unskilled and uneducated, had unwittingly trapped themselves in a never-ending cycle. Their potential earning power kept dwindling, and their ability to achieve better incomes kept falling, but at the same time they could see the continual rise of the elite and the educated. As the working class went without, the elite enjoyed abundance—even affluence, attending soirées and recitals, dressing in finery, dining on Christmas turkeys and other delicacies, and indulging their children with gifts, nannies, and governesses. The elite lived in exclusive locations like Kensington or Westminster. Even the educated fared better than the masses, receiving jobs as managers and foremen, whilst the working class slaved away, with blackened faces and lungs full of coal dust.

Innocence Lost—Children of Coal

Before long, people began to notice the huge divide amongst classes—especially the difference in earnings and level of comfort. This prevailing trend then gave birth to the most popular advice most of us received from our parents: "My child, if you want to be successful in life, don't be like your old mum or dad! Please stay in school and get a good education. Go to university so you'll get a good job." During the Industrial Revolution—and well through the twentieth century—this advice made a lot of sense. A focus on education and jobs for the masses had been established, meaning that the masses had no further interest in entrepreneurism. As a result, the class divide was now complete: the ordinary people got jobs, and the rich went into business.

Human society, however, continued to change and evolve through technological and scientific discoveries. The more our society evolved, the more things changed socially and economically. Today's world has no actual memory of the Industrial Revolution. We have fully entered the Information Age.

The old advice of go to school, get a good education, and then get a good job doesn't work anymore. Unlike the times of the Industrial Revolution where 95 per cent of the work force spent the day crammed into factories and coal mines because that was the labour demand of the day, employment today remains in a state of flux. The average person will change jobs about fifteen to twenty times throughout their lives, for reasons that could range from redundancies to dismissals. Yet most still believe that job security actually exists. Every year our universities turn out 300,000 new graduates, according to the BBC News (BBC News website "Q&A All Doom and Gloom for Graduates?" 14/01/09). Does this mean that there must be 300,000 new posts waiting to be snapped up by these new graduates? Sadly, it does not. Now imagine that these new graduates all have identical qualifications from different universities, so they are essentially vying for the same jobs. Add to that the fact that if there are not that many jobs to go round, what happens to the 300,000 new graduates waiting to join the workforce the following year, and the year after that? Most of us know someone who's got a degree from a university but works in a fast-food restaurant.

The linear income is almost redundant in today's world. It has no security built into it, although many might think that it does. The ability to earn is totally dependent on the availability to work, which means that if you are unable to work because of sickness, family emergencies, or death you cannot earn an income. If your employer can no longer support a workforce due to bankruptcies or mergers and acquisitions, once again your ability to earn stops. In short, if you don't clock the time you can't earn the money, as linear income depends on your fulfilling the time obligation.

The Linear Income

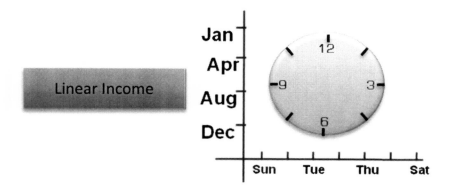

The figure above shows the principal components of linear income: the calendar and the clock. We are all quite familiar with the term "nine-to-five job". It does not really matter how much you earn in wages when you receive your pay based on an hourly rate or annual salary, wages are seldom paid according to your skills but according to actual time spent working. If you don't believe me, don't go to work for a couple of months, even days, without permission—see what happens. The people who earn money this way are employees working from nine to five. The self-employed also work based on time, but their clients or projects usually dictate the amount of time they spend working. Retailers earn money when they are open for business; this includes owners of restaurants, malls, or small shops. Regardless of what type of establishment they own, their income stops when the shop is closed for business.

Linear income is mostly self-centred because it has no long-term benefits; when you get a job regardless of the size of your wage packet, you leave nothing behind should anything happen to you. How many families are there, I wonder, that have found themselves in this situation? The main income earner dies after having worked hard for many years to build his linear income to an impressive annual wage, providing the house, the car, and private education for his children, whilst the wife remained at home looking after the children. As a result of his death, the family loses the home, the car, and the exclusive education; the widow cannot expect her late husband's employers to continue paying his wages, which he had earned based on an hourly rate or annual salary. In other words: **if he can't get to work, he doesn't get paid.** No long-term security exists in the linear income.

Leveraged Income

This is stage two of the IGS, and its primary building block is numbers. Leveraged income allows people to harness the power of numbers and make that power work to their advantage. This is called **leveraging.** Imagine you're in a tug of war. Your team has 200 men, whilst the opposing team has 50 men. Elementary deduction will conclude that the obvious victors in that game will be the team with more numbers on their side.

The linear income relies on the sole responsibility of one person, whereas the leveraged income requires the collaboration of many; in short, it's a numbers game. Imagine if you could go to work every day and earn £100.00; next, imagine you could clone yourself 100 times, with each clone working to earn £100.00 per day. Your daily income would be in excess of £10,000.00 per day (PD), and this is the advantage of leveraging—a simple profitable equation also known as networking!

In the words of Robert Kiyosaki: "The richest people in the world build networks. Everyone else is trained to look for work."

$$\text{You x £100.00 PD = £100.00 PD}$$

$$\text{OR}$$

$$\text{You x 100 Clones x £100.00 PD = £10,000.00 PD}$$

Every major corporation on the planet understands this principle: if you want to make more money, you need leverage. Building leverage income allows you to naturally incorporate safety into your income. For example, let's return to the cloning idea for a moment. Imagine that three of your clones meet with an unfortunate accident on their way to work, thus removing them from the equation: you would still have 70 per cent of your income coming in. However, if you alone provide your (linear) income, and then you meet with an accident or sustain some misfortune, you will lose 100 per cent of your (linear) income, as will your dependents.

The Leveraged Income

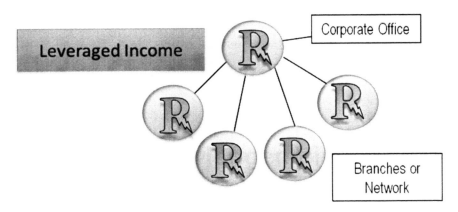

The figure above shows a typical corporate franchise network, such as McDonald's, Burger King, or Pizza Hut. There is usually a central office, or headquarters, that the franchisee may have to approach in order to buy into the franchise. Thousands, or even tens of thousands, of these exist today, and they largely utilise the leverage principle to earn their income. If just the main offices of these companies existed, without the franchises, they would not have had the ability to reach as many people as they have; thus, they wouldn't have earned the kind of income that they have. Let's take a closer look at a few of these.

McDonald's Corporation (Restaurant Group): More than 32,000 locations globally; headquarters in Oak Brook, Illinois, USA; revenue 2010 $24.08 billion.

Burger King (Restaurant Group): More than 12,200 outlets in 73 countries; headquarters in Miami, Florida, USA; revenue 2010 $2.5 billion.

Virgin Atlantic (part of Virgin Airways): Fleet size 32 with 29-plus on order base of operation Gatwick and Heathrow airports; headquarters Crawley, UK; revenue 2010 £2.38 billion.

Barclays Bank PLC (Global Banking Corporation): World's tenth-largest banking and financial services group, as of 2010; headquarters Canary Wharf, UK; global operations in more than fifty countries and territories across Africa, Asia, Europe, North America, and South America, with approximately 48 million customers; revenue 2010 £29.955 billion; total assets £1.38 trillion.

The list goes on. All these companies made impressive incomes because they leveraged the potential of their income; they used the power of numbers. Billionaire Jean Paul Getty said, "I would rather earn 1 per cent off 100 people's efforts than 100 per cent off my own efforts." However, the issue for many people is not knowing how to tap into the leverage principles in order to begin realising these potential benefits for themselves and their own incomes.

The truth is actually quite simple: leverage is built on networking—that is "cloning" your business. Firstly, you create a corporate identity, put a product in place, create a system of marketing and distribution, and then implement what I'd like to call "operation cookie cutter"—i.e., you make as many copies (clones) as you can and transplant them all around the world. Now, to do this on your own would probably cost you millions, maybe even billions, however, to achieve a similar result without the astronomical cost, there are other methods that can be utilised such as network marketing.

Network marketing is a business model that allows the individual to harness the same leverage principles as the large corporations do, but on a personal level with people he or she knows, such as friends, family members, and acquaintances. Rather than investing capital in assets, logistics, and a workforce, the individual would only need to concentrate his or her effort on training one other person. That person, in turn, learns by means of training and then passes on that learning to the next person, and so on. The results can be absolutely outstanding, and quite often they are. In network marketing, you become the central office, and every new person who joins your team becomes your new branch manager or franchisee (personal franchise or network). Equally as impressive as building a multimillion-dollar corporation, many of the financial gurus today have admitted that if they had it to do over again, they would most certainly build their businesses based on network marketing. The challenging issue has always been that people do not understand the power of this business model.

How Network Marketing Generates Income

I have been in network marketing for about nine years now, and I can say it's more popular today than it was when I began—or even than it was five years ago. I personally know many people who swore that they would never touch multilevel marketing (MLM)—even with a barge pole—yet today they are involved in MLM and doing quite well. Change is the most constant thing in the universe; given time, everything and everyone changes.

The business principles that govern network marketing or MLM are simple, familiar, and easy to understand; however, mixing human beings into the equation really complicates things. When people see the business model for the first time they tend to always think of two

43

things: (1) how much money they could possibly make, and (2) what products the company manufactures. Although the presentation usually includes a bunch of other things like selling, recommending the products to friends and family, and creating a customer base, by the end of the presentation most people have erased these points from their minds, focusing on the two above-captioned items. This naturally creates a problem for new distributors, as they start to realise that you can't make money just by signing up new distributors, and certainly you can't make money if you refuse to sell or self-use the products. Before we go any further, let's take a quick look at how this system works.

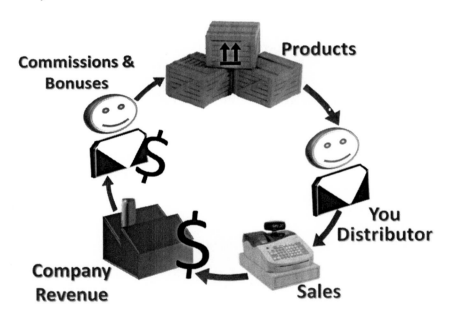

The Products

Let's start with the products, as this is usually how most people would initially come in contact with multilevel marketing. Statistically, through my own personal experience talking with people in my training programmes and seminars, I have learned that approximately 70 per cent of people involved in MLM today first learned about it either by having been a customer (user of the product) or by having friends introduce them to using the product as a means of contact (networking or referral). Secondly, by law—and this applies to every country on the planet that has come to recognise MLM as a legitimate business—working with the Direct Selling Association (DSA), as a global regulating authority in the industry, it has been accepted that without a product line or some sort of service of value to support the business, the opportunity will be regarded as an illegal pyramid system. So you can't have network marketing or MLM without a product line. The product line ensures that the payment structure or compensation plan is based on revenues created through product sales; sometimes secondary opportunities to generate income arise as well.

The Distributor

In this system, the distributor is you—or members of your team, such as friends, family members, or colleagues from work. You are all individual business owners/distributors who receive individual commissions to generate sales by leveraging (taking advantage of) the unique, sometimes exclusive, nature of the company's product line. You will be expected to **always** create a monthly minimum turnover in **points value.** This is where MLM comes into its own, because when each distributor individually creates a minimum volume turnover in his or her business, the organisation collectively benefits (i.e., a distributor who has invested extra time and effort in creating and training his or her team with proper duplication in place will be able to leverage a larger points turnover. Thus, through MLM, one distributor's minimum volume turnover can create thousands, or even tens of thousands, of sales volume, which could result in earnings of six figures or more.

Sales

It's important to bear in mind that it's the sale of product that creates the income. When distributors carry out their commission to generate sales by creating a healthy customer base, and also using their own products and encouraging their team to do the same, everyone will benefit. But things do not always work out this way, and that is simply because the new distributor hasn't yet understood the principle, hasn't made the commitment required to be successful in the business, and/or is having difficulties finding customers. These are issues that can easily be fixed through personal development and training. Finally, sales also create a profit for the distributor; this is usually based on a margin calculated from the difference between the wholesale and retail sale of the products.

The Company's Revenue

Distributors' sales activities create sales volume, and sales volume creates revenue for the MLM company that supports you; commissions are paid from this, and also the revenue allows the company to be able to develop more and better products and services. Some companies present their distributors with a global network marketing opportunity, with products and services available in most countries around the world. As a result, these companies can generate millions, even billions, of sales annually.

Commissions and Bonuses

Network marketing companies don't generally advertise their products through conventional advertising channels, as these are usually costly and wasteful; most companies are able to pay out six-figure bonuses to their distributors. Commissions and bonuses are paid out of sales revenue, and sometimes out of the advertising budget; hence, MLM companies can afford to pay quite a handsome sum to distributors. Unfortunately, many who begin never experience this benefit because they tend to sabotage their own success by refusing to learn and utilise the business systems—or are just simply not ready to make the single-minded commitment required to achieve success. If this cycle breaks down at any point, it would be hard for the distributor to accomplish his or her goal hence impossible to develop an effective leverage income

Residual Income

The third and final stage of IGS, residual income is long-term income also known as cash flow and passive income. Passive income involves a two-part process. The active part describes the period when you started putting the building blocks in place to create this income—the genesis of your enterprise. This might take anywhere from three to five years to accomplish; ten years in some instances. During this period you will have to finance your business, invest time, and expend a lot of effort. The passive stage is the period when your business starts to pay you back for your past efforts, allowing you to live your dreams and passively enjoy the fruits of your labour—even though you're no longer working hard to build the business, as you already accomplished that in the past. The trouble is, many people do not want to wait that long; they have no patience, so they settle for a job instead, as this allows them to spend their wages on things that give them immediate gratification.

The Residual Income

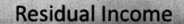 

Understanding the mechanisms that control this income is crucial. If not for my mentor, Jaz Hanspal, who pointed all of this out to me, I would still be in a job today. I can never thank him enough for the six years he dedicated to working with me, challenging and moulding my mind, which made me who I am today. Of course, many others contributed to my financial education over the years, but it was Jaz who worked with me in the trenches. I learned that it was more profitable to build a pipeline than to carry buckets of water, because you only need to do the work once—you may have to invest time, money, blood, sweat, and guts; but once it's done, it's done forever. (For more on this idea, I suggest you read one of the first books recommended to me, *Parable of the Pipeline* by Burke Hedges.)

Another way to look at this is by means of this comparison. Imagine that you own a piece of land and you have decided to plant corn. That would seem to be a good idea, as you obviously will receive a rather bountiful return: one seed of corn yields a stalk with five to six ears of corn, an average of 2,000 to 3,000 seeds per stalk (rough estimate). However, the downside is that you would have to replant the field every year in order to get an annual harvest. However, if you planted an orchard or a vineyard on your land instead, you would only have to do the work once but would get the result, or harvest, continually, year after year.

Most network marketing and MLM systems allow you to earn residual income, which means you could dedicate a few years to building your organisation, and then you would be able to retire—live the life you really want, doing the things you really want. With some network marketing companies today you can will your income to your children; so in essence, you are building a legacy when you build your residual income. These days it's rare to find anyone working towards this principle; people are born, they grow up, get an education, get a job, and then die. The only legacy most people leave behind is an ugly mountain of debt. In past centuries, parents worked hard to build their own businesses so they could leave their children an inheritance; these days, most parents relish the day they move in with their children, arguing that it is only fair because they conceived and raised the children, enduring all the sacrifices along the way, and now it's the children's turn to return the favour.

The job culture has left society totally barren. No man fights for honour and integrity anymore; every man's just out for himself. The prevailing attitude is, "As long as I'm OK, who cares about society or culture?" Or perhaps it's just that we have just lost touch with the basics and need to get back to those ancient principles.

Enterprise over Slavery

In the passage at the beginning of this chapter Jacob made a decision that was enterprising, with long-term benefits and positive consequences for himself and his family. Jaz taught me the value of looking to the future rather than focusing on instant gratification. It happened after he'd given me some advice—details I can't recall anymore. My response was a little silly; I told him that I couldn't do what he'd asked because "it just wasn't my thing".

He replied, "Daniel! When you go shopping every month, do you only shop for yourself, or do you consider your entire family?"

"My entire family, of course," I answered.

My mentor replied, "So why won't you carry out my instructions? Do you not think it's a bit lame to make a silly excuse like 'it's not my thing'? Can you not see that the financial reward will benefit you and your family in the long-term?"

Laban kept insisting on making Jacob a job offer, trying to get him to agree to a wage, but Jacob would have none of it. Instead, he favoured a business deal. Jacob said to Laban *Now it's time for me to start looking out for my own family*. In short, "I need to build a legacy. I need to think of the long-term rather than the instant gratification." *I don't want you to pay me anything.* That is, "I don't want a job or wage." If Jacob had settled for a job or wage, he would likely have received the minimum—perhaps just enough to make sure that he'd come to depend on that pittance, and then he would have been stuck at Laban's for the rest of his life, doing all the work whilst Laban reaped all the benefits. This is a bit like the workforce today, or even during the Industrial Revolution some 150 to 200 years ago. Nothing has really changed; the working class will always draw the short straw. Jacob negotiated a deal that meant he could get a residual benefit for all he had done for Laban. Jacob built his pipeline, and then he was able to sit back in retirement, assured that his pipeline (flock) would generate a continuous cash flow that he could leave to the next generation.

In *The Perfect Business*, Robert Kiyosaki puts this another way: "My poor dad says work hard, but my rich dad says why would you work hard for something you'll never own and you can get fired from right away? It makes more sense to work hard to build a business, something you own and something you can pass on from generation to generations to your kids."

Chapter 6

THE PRINCIPLE

Indecision Is a Guaranteed Decision to Fail

James 1:6-8 (Common English Bible)
Whoever asks shouldn't hesitate. They should ask in faith, without doubting. Whoever doubts is like the surf of the sea, tossed and turned by the wind. People like that should never imagine that they will receive anything from the LORD. They are double-minded, unstable in all their ways.

An ancient African proverb says, "If there is no enemy within, the enemy without can do you no harm." The most formidable adversaries we will ever have to face in our lives are the negative voices within each of us, the conversations we endlessly have with ourselves. We recognise these voices as our own and so we become familiar and comfortable with them, offering little to no resistance to the suggestions they present. We will convince ourselves that no one knows us better than we know ourselves, so if our familiar voice says we can't do stuff, it would be silly to argue against it. Besides, people might think you're crazy if you go around arguing with yourself. Lewis Pugh wrote, "There is nothing more powerful than a made-up mind." The negative conversations in our minds are designed to invoke only one response from us: petrifaction! In geological science, this refers to a phenomenon in which organic matter is turned into stone. It's like the Greek myths that told of men turning to stone after looking into the eyes of a Gorgon. For a more contemporary image, it's like a deer caught in the headlamps of an oncoming car, asking inwardly if he should run or stay put. In

53

the midst of the deer's momentary hesitation, the driver slams on the brakes, resulting in roadkill. Petrifaction never yields a positive outcome!

A made-up mind is focused and determined; above all, little or no background noise goes on within it to distract that focus and determination. The made-up mind is calm, and the person who possesses such a mind has learned to focus his energy on the task at hand. However, such a mind is not entirely quiet; it does have internal conversations going on, but these conversations rarely contradict the intension at hand. The internal conversations of the person possessing a made-up mind are positive, congruent with the visions, beliefs, dreams, and goals that the individual has set. Such a person will neither be moved nor shaken.

One of my favourite TV programmes was *Star Trek: Voyager*. Unfortunately, the series isn't on any longer, however, I often recall a profound quote by the character Seven of Nine: "When your captain first approached us we suspected that an agreement with humans would prove impossible to maintain. You are erratic, conflicted, disorganised. Every decision is debated, every action questioned. Every individual entitled to their own small opinion. You lack harmony, cohesion, greatness. It will be your undoing." (*Star Trek: Voyager* "Scorpions")

This quote highlights nine deep-rooted reasons for human failure:

> We are erratic.
> We are conflicted.
> We are disorganised.
> We debate every decision.
> We question every action.
> We each are entitled to our own small opinion.
> We lack harmony.
> We lack cohesion.
> We lack greatness.

The above-captioned nine reasons lead to our "undoing" (i.e., failure).

Quite a bit like the British Parliament during the prime minister's question time. Imagine all this conflict or noise is actually carrying on in a person's mind, and as if that weren't enough, many would additionally invite their friends' and neighbours' negative opinions. Inviting a coalition of negative-thinking friends into your head—who will deceive you into thinking they're helping by encouraging you not to fail—only ensures that you will do nothing, because all they do is discourage you from doing anything. You see, you can't fail if you do nothing! They will tell you what you already know from your internal conversations: "forget it"; "you can't do it"; "it'll never work"; "don't be crazy"; and so on. Remember, they are having the same issues in their own minds; they are trapped in the same loop.

How to Make Quality Decisions

Find someone who is in the place in life where you want to be, and then emulate that person. We need to understand the importance of coaches and mentors. Such individuals are absolutely essential, and it is natural throughout our lives, from childhood to adulthood, to have someone to look up to. We see this in sports and business all the time. Mentors made a difference in my life. Those who made the most impact in my life were my business mentors: Jaz Hanspal, Jerry Scriven, and a few others. I have already discussed Jaz. As I said, he was with me from the beginning, helping me build myself from the ground up. Jaz lived just a few minutes away from me, and I remember many meetings and business counselling sessions that helped me grow my entrepreneurial backbone. Jerry Scriven was a very successful multimillionaire and entrepreneur; I knew I wanted to be like him. Others I admired influenced me as well; they were more like "surrogate mentors", because I did not have access to them personally. I made up my mind to follow their teaching and guidance by listening to their wisdom and studying their works. These are people like Les Brown, Zig Ziglar, Stephen Covey, and Fred Harties, just to name a few. I read their books, attended their seminars, and waited to speak with them afterwards, hoping for some tidbit of information—a wise word to help me move forward.

This was obviously a long process. Jaz once asked me to think about a seemingly simple image: If you put a blot of black paint into a bucket of white paint, would the paint remain white? How much more white paint would you need to make that paint in the bucket return to complete whiteness? The answer is: a lot. I have heard many people suggest that reading books and attending seminars is akin to brainwashing. If you consider that most of us, when we were younger, had bigger dreams and higher expectations of ourselves—we all wanted to achieve greatness to go to the stars—but by the time we reached adulthood we had lost our enthusiasm, we had become cynical, bitter, and doubtful. So what happened to our younger selves? Would it be correct if I suggested that we had been "brainwashed" to become less of who we all started out to be through a lifetime of negative "seminars" from our own internal conversations and our environment? People constantly suggesting that we will amount to nothing because: we are too stupid; we have no college education; we are black, white, Hispanic, or whatever else their own bias precludes from success; we are single parents, drug addicts, or ex-convicts; and on and on. Isn't this the same "seminar" or conversation we have been having inside our own heads? So we have already been brainwashed to think we are failures—what harm would it do to be brainwashed to start believing in ourselves again?

Quality decisions come from a quality mind. "Garbage in, garbage out" (GIGO), as the saying goes. How can people expect to rule their own destinies when they have no real substance within them?

Out of the abundance of the heart the mouth speaks.
[Matthew 12:34]

In order to make quality decisions, we have to saturate our minds and environment with quality information, from quality people, books, and other influences. Then and only then can we truly control our destinies.

As William Ernest Henley wrote in "Invictus":

> "It matters not how strait the gate,
> How charged with punishments the scroll,
> I am the master of my fate:
> I am the captain of my soul."

To recover the reins and resume control of our own lives we need to unify our internal conversations and develop a single, positive voice that we listen to. Like a laser beam, we each have to focus on what we want and the long-term outcomes and consequences of our decisions. A double-minded man is unstable in all his ways; this describes a condition known as **schism**, which signifies a rupture, split, or disunity. People sometimes say to themselves, "I am of two minds: should I stay or should I go?" Unable to decide, they freeze like the deer in the headlamps. Everything shuts down, and that is the root of indecision and failure. **Not making a decision is not the same as avoiding failure.** There is no middle ground—you win or you lose.

Chapter 7

THE PRINCIPLE

Wisdom Is the
Path to Wealth

1 Kings 4:29-35 (Amplified Bible)
*And God gave Solomon exceptionally much wisdom
and understanding, and breadth of mind like the sand
of the seashore.*

*Solomon's wisdom excelled the wisdom of all the people
of the East and all the wisdom of Egypt. For he was
wiser than all other men—than Ethan the Ezrahite,
and Heman, Calcol, and Darda, the sons of Mahol.
His fame was in all the nations round about. He also
originated 3,000 proverbs, and his songs were 1,005.
He spoke of trees, from the cedar that is in Lebanon to
the hyssop that grows out of the wall; he spoke also of
beasts, of birds, of creeping things, and of fish. Men
came from all peoples to hear the wisdom of Solomon,
and from all kings of the earth who had heard of his
wisdom.*

1 Kings 10:23-29
*So King Solomon exceeded all the kings of the earth in
riches and in wisdom (skill).*

*And all the earth sought the presence of Solomon to
hear his wisdom which God had put in his mind.
Every man brought tribute: vessels of silver and gold,
garments, equipment, spices, horses, and mules, so
much year by year.*

Solomon collected chariots and horsemen; he had 1,400 chariots and 12,000 horsemen, which he stationed in the chariot cities and with the king in Jerusalem.

The king made silver as common in Jerusalem as stones, and cedars as plentiful as the sycamore trees in the lowlands.
Solomon's horses were brought out of Egypt, and the king's merchants received them in droves, each at a price.

A chariot could be brought out of Egypt for 600 shekels of silver, and a horse for 150. And so to all the kings of the Hittites and of Syria they were exported by the king's merchants.

Jim Rohn once said, "Income seldom exceeds personal development." This statement is so profoundly accurate that we can quantify the many successful entrepreneurs and business owners who rose to success in this modern age by it. There are two kinds of education you can obtain today: formal education and personal development. They are quite different from one another in both their format and delivery.

Formal education, as we all know, is delivered in a classroom or lecture theatre environment (or online version thereof), and is usually supported by a system of quality control which requires the students to be regularly tested and graded. Formal education is primarily designed to be academic in delivery; it largely focuses on equipping and developing a labour force which is expected to be academically qualified in a field of expertise. This means a potential employer could have confidence in the skill sets of his employees, given that the expert employees already in the labour force are suitably qualified. With this system, students are expected to finish their education and then join the work force.

In addition, formal education has inadvertently had some unexpected adverse social and psychological effects on today's society. Firstly, many have experienced feelings of inferiority when, for various reasons, they failed to complete their formal education to the highest level. A silent code exists by which those who might be considered "semi-educated" experience discrimination of sorts; that is, those who are well educated look down on those whom they think are not well educated. This creates a two-tiered society, where those considered "learned" are proud to speak openly of their knowledge and qualifications, and those who are not are ashamed to admit to the fact that they never acquired a higher level of qualification.

This trend is more pronounced in certain African and Asian cultures. Having grown up in Nigeria, I witnessed this trend first-hand. Nigerian parents feel proud talking about their "graduate" children; they boast about their qualifications in medicine, law, and engineering. Everyone in Nigeria wants their kids to be engineers, lawyers, or doctors, but no one is interested in knowing what the poor kid really wants to do. Tens of thousands are spent these days in educating children to considerably high levels, which may even include master's and/or doctorate programmes, resulting in twenty-plus years of education overall. However, this offers no guarantee of a job at the end, but entails an education that costs close to a king's ransom. Someone is making money, but it's not the students—it's the schools. The average foreign student in the UK will spend about £12,000.00 per term, and many must work—sometimes illegally—to meet their living costs. The parents also have to work very hard in order to raise the necessary funds to keep paying this ransom of tuition, but they can't imagine any other possible alternative to formal education.

Recently I was in Glasgow conducting a meeting on business opportunities, and I met two engineering students from Bangladesh completing their master's degrees at Glasgow University. After the meeting they both decided to join the programme. I invited them for a chat at my hotel that afternoon, as I was leaving to return to

England the following day. I started by asking the usual questions, just trying to get to know them better, and I learned that they both were taking postgraduate courses in hydro-engineering. I asked why they wanted to start their own business, and they said that they just wanted to make a little bit of money to help with the economic hardship of funding their education. They delivered leaflets in the evenings just to earn money. Hearing that, I asked them how much their tuition was per term. I was shocked to learn that they had to pay £14,000.00 per term for a two-year course of study. I couldn't understand why anyone would do that to themselves.

So I asked them this very important question, "If I wrote you each a cheque for £28,000.00 right now, what would you do with it? Would you run off to a university and enrol yourself on a postgraduate course, or would you invest it in a profitable business?" They both said that if they had that money right now they would invest it.

It seems to me that most people do not think too deeply about why they do the things that they do anymore. Instead they seem compelled to carry out these orders: "Go to school, get a good education, go to university, and then get a good job."

On August 2nd 2009 the *New York Post* published a report on a twenty-seven-year-old graduate student who had filed a lawsuit at the Bronx Supreme Court against Monroe College, because the school had not done enough to find her a job. She'd spent $70,000.00 to attend the programme and obtain the degree, but then she could not find a job.

I neither agree nor disagree with this situation meriting a lawsuit; I merely present it as an example. Nor am I against formal education. What I disagree with is the notion that it provides all the answers and means to success, whilst evidence has shown that many wealthy people today do much better in life financially simply because they tend to invest in a different sort of education. Evidence also shows that even those with a good formal education only start changing their financial situation once they start to embrace personal development.

What Is Personal Development?

Some call it "success education", and many people, me included, believe that it offers almost scientific proof that as a result of acquiring it anyone can create positive results and achieve success. That is, those who commit to personal development will realise success in all they do, every single time—the results are as predictable as carrying out an experiment in a laboratory.

I believe that if you take any successful, self-made millionaires, strip them of all their assets, and then drop them off naked on any continent, as long as other people live on that same continent, within five years those former millionaires will be wealthy, and within ten years they will be millionaires again. You can do this over and over, again and again, and the "experiment" will yield the same results every single time. Most millionaires have been bankrupt at least once in their lives, most famous being Donald Trump, who was a multibillionaire at the time of his bankruptcy, and who is a billionaire again—twice in one lifetime—and yet, many people struggle to make significant dent on their financial challenges.

So how do these self-made successes do it? Success leaves clues. What will you find most successful people doing on a very regular basis? Reading! You will find them reading constantly, and I'm not talking about textbooks but success-focused books. If they are not reading such books, they are writing their own. A few examples include Robert Kiyosaki's *Rich Dad* publications, and also *Why We Want You to Be Rich*, which he co-authored with Donald Trump; *Think and Grow Rich* by Napoleon Hill, an all-time best-seller (seventy years and counting); *The Magic of Thinking Big* by David J. Schwartz; and the list goes on. Hardly a single successful self-made millionaire today exists who hasn't read at least one of these books; many of them read the books before they became successful, or at least will tell you that reading the books contributed largely towards their success in some shape or form. These successful people also invest large sums of their money in their personal development, attending seminars and conferences, and watching and/or listening to DVDs and CDs. Sometimes they themselves run these seminars and conferences—and/or produce the audios and videos—all to help empower others seeking to achieving the same results that they already have attained. As I said earlier, the results can be duplicated by anyone who has the right information. The trouble is, most people have no interest in this sort of education, because they do not think it has any "status". Sadly, many today prefer to have status than to be rich or successful.

The Wisdom of Solomon

Most people have heard of King Solomon in some form or other, or they have read about him, his wisdom, his diamond mines, and his fairness in executing judgment. However not many people actually think deeply enough about King Solomon to make the connection between his wealth and his wisdom.

> **1Kings 10:23-25**
> *So **King Solomon exceeded all the kings of the earth in riches and in wisdom** (skill).*
>
> *And all the earth sought the presence of Solomon to hear his wisdom which God had put in his mind. **Every man brought tribute: vessels of silver and gold, garments, equipment, spices, horses, and mules, so much year by year.***

Let's take another look at the above passage. It seems like people—kings and rulers everywhere—paid just to hear Solomon speak. The stories go on and on, and throughout the passages it is quite clear and evident that a direct relationship existed between Solomon's vast wealth and his wisdom. Solomon never received any formal education (universities did not exist in ancient times). Palace tutors would have schooled him whilst he was growing up, but beyond that he must have been very observant and curious by nature; he would have been open to all types of learning and to searching to discover the truth of all things, rather than pursuing a single discipline. Above all, he would have surrendered himself as mentee to the wise mentors, which would definitely have included his father, King David.

The point is, Solomon's wisdom was unconventional; hence, he could think outside the box. He was always poised and relaxed in his mental attitude at all times, because his mind was sound—that is, built on a solid foundation of personal development motivated by his natural inclination to curiosity. All this becomes quite evident in the book of Ecclesiastes, where the reader gains a glimpse into the unique mind of a great king and leader.

Knowledge versus Wisdom

Proverbs 24:14
In the same way, wisdom is sweet to your soul. If you find it, you will have a bright future, and your hopes will not be cut short.

Now let's consider the above verse from Proverbs, along with what we've already discussed about Solomon. The ancient Greeks used two different words to refer to knowledge and wisdom, just as we do in English. However, when translating these words into English, it is a common mistake to use one for the other, colloquially. In truth, in ancient Greek as well as in English, these words are very different and bear separate meanings.

The Greek word for **knowledge** is "oida", meaning "to see"; it is a perfect tense with a present meaning, signifying, primarily, "to have seen or perceived"; hence, "to know, to have knowledge of". As in the case of human "knowledge", to know from observation or study. However, the Greek word for **wisdom** is "sophia", which signifies "to have insight into the true nature of all things". This describes Solomon. It is also what sets personal development apart from mere cerebral education. Those who engage in personal development are open to learning all kinds of things, and they seek to understand all things with objectivity. Most people who consider formal education important only rely on the status derived from their qualifications.

They are mostly subjective in their thinking, and their favourite comments are usually things like, "I am a doctor—lawyer, engineer, or whichever credential applies—and I don't have time for that sort of thing." They put themselves in a little box marked "doctor", "lawyer", "engineer", etc., seal the box, and then never think about anything outside that box. They rarely see or understand the point of personal development, or building businesses like network marketing or MLM, unless they decide to delve into personal development or **wisdom.**

[**AUTHOR'S NOTE:** *For those who have never explored the avenue of personal development but who would like to get started, please refer to the page entitled "Recommended Books and Audio" at the end of this book.*]

Chapter 8

THE PRINCIPLE

Action Creates Results

> **Matthew 7:7-8** (New Living Translation)
> *Keep on asking, and you will receive what you ask for.*
> *Keep on seeking, and you will find. Keep on knocking,*
> *and the door will be opened to you.* [8] *For everyone who*
> *asks, receives. Everyone who seeks, finds. And to*
> *everyone who knocks, the door will be opened.*

Many people do not take action because they are afraid of failure. In their judgment, misguided though it is, they believe that if they don't take any action they cannot possibly fail. Obviously, this way of thinking is greatly flawed. On this planet (it may be different on other planets, so I won't conjecture!) the only way to change one's circumstances—or encourage a desired result in one's life—is to take action. Refusing to take action and basing that decision on the fear of failure can only guarantee one result: **failure!** Refusing to take action is a guarantee of failure; in other words, inaction is the same as deciding to fail. It is amazing how many people do not realise this; you cannot protect yourself from failing, but you can prevent yourself from succeeding. If you do not succeed in life it is because you have not taken action.

A number of years ago my wife, Terri, had a very unpleasant experience at work. She was a manager vying for promotion, and on the day of the interviews, she had sought a colleague's advice on interviewing skills. The well-meaning friend advised Terri that all she had to watch out for, or avoid doing, in an interview was saying "errrm" or "errrs". Well, you guessed it, as soon as the interviewer asked the first question, Terri immediately said, "errrm". From that point on the entire interview went downhill. Terri told me this story quite a while after it happened, but the most poignant thing she said about it was that in her mind as soon as she said "errrm", she immediately remembered what her colleague had warned her about—that it would be the worst thing she could say or do in an interview—and she felt that she had failed big time. Once she thought that, every time she opened her mouth during the interview, all she could say was "errrm".

Now, many would respond to this by saying, "That didn't go too well, but get over it and move on." Unfortunately, the incident actually had a secondary negative effect on Terri that was totally unexpected. As a result of that one event, Terri suddenly found that she could not bear to be in front of an audience speaking: she had inadvertently developed a fear of public speaking. She could not bear to be in front of any crowd—or even one person—if she had to be the one speaking. As long as attention was on her, she would fall to pieces. She told me that on the same day that she had fumbled her interview, another manager asked her to assist in interviewing some new job applicants. The interview was going quite well, with her colleague asking all the questions. But when her colleague asked Terri to explain her area of expertise with the company to the candidate, Terri's first response again was, "errrm". Psychologically she fell to pieces, even though now the role was reversed: she was conducting the interview. Nevertheless, that was the beginning of her fear of public speaking. The final act came about when a senior manager brought a client round to Terri's desk, asking her to explain how an IT tool worked. She did so, but she told me that she could feel her voice trembling through the entire presentation and convinced herself that the client could hear it too. After the client left, Terri called her manager, crying on the phone and complaining about how the senior manager had embarrassed her in the presence of a client.

Terri's Victory

In April 2010, about four years after Terri's nightmare experience, I enrolled both of us in a public-speaking course at (SpeakersKey) run by Hanieh Chehrehnegari, who has since become a very good friend of ours, and who wrote the foreword for this book. I saw Terri battle her fears for two whole days, but in the end she emerged victorious. **Action creates results!** To put this another way, **if you fail to take action, you fail.** At the end of the two-day course, another one of my mentors, Bernie De Souza, who was a surprise keynote speaker for the event, encouraged us each to write down our goals for the next thirty days.

Terri's written goal was to arrange to speak at our daughter's secondary school, to the year tens and elevens. As soon as we got back from the event, she wasted no time in contacting the school; she didn't give her fear an opportunity to gain a foothold again, and she didn't allow herself to make her next decision from a position of weakness.

Terri set up the speaking event almost immediately; in fact, everything went through so fast that from our return home following the two-day course to Terri's speaking event at the school, only about ten days passed. Terri received very good feedback from the school and the kids who attended, and she has never looked back. She now speaks regularly at various events that we hold in the UK.

How Much Action Is Enough Action?

There is no such thing as "enough action"! Thinking that you have taken enough action would be the same as thinking that you would someday stop growing. The only time to stop taking action is when you die, which is also the only time you stop growing. Although only one of the two activities in this case is voluntary, as you actually can decide to do nothing to change your life, but you cannot decide not to die. Nevertheless, choosing to do nothing to change your life is a condition that I describe as "dead but awaiting the funeral".

The principle that governs the process of action and result is actually formatted to automatically produce recurring positive results, sometimes even indefinitely. This principle is known as the **results triangle.** The triangle starts at its pinnacle with **motivation,** or your reason why. In other words, you have to examine and define why you need the results you are seeking in your life. For Terri, it was the feelings of helplessness and unhappiness that she always faced whenever she had to stand before a crowd. She didn't like these feelings and wanted to change them, so her **motivation**—her reason for taking action or her "motive-for-action"—was influenced by negative emotions, things she didn't want to feel. Motivation does not have to come from a negative. You can also be influenced by a positive emotion—something you do want—call it your dream, if you prefer that emotion.

The next point on the triangle is **action.** Once you have decided on what you do or do not want—your reason why; your motivation—you then make that realisation your launching pad, using it to propel you into action. Be aware that you have to accomplish this quickly, before the negative internal conversation starts, drawing your energy away from your reason why. You must take action before you start telling yourself things like, "I can't have that!"; "What am I thinking?"; "Why am I fooling myself?"; and so on. (You know those conversations; I covered them in chapter 6.) Don't dwell on those conversations now; move past them! I'm showing you how you can get results simply by understanding just how powerful taking action can be. You do not have to be afraid of failure, and you no longer need to prevent yourself from getting what you really want. The key is to take action quickly, just as Terri did after she attended the seminar. In short, when you take action you will get results, and that is the third stage of the process. The third point of the triangle is **results.**

Results Triangle

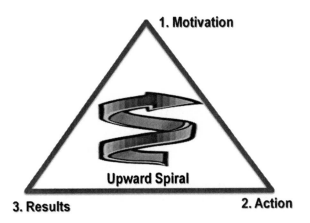

1. Motivation

Upward Spiral

3. Results   **2. Action**

When you take action and get a positive result, you will feel good about yourself; you will feel proud that you have accomplished something. Above all, you will recognise that you have just faced your worst fear and overcome it. You will feel triumphant because you will realise that over time your previous condition of fear came to rule you, making you weaker and weaker. Once you realise all this, you will become even more motivated as a result of your accomplishments; thus, you will continue to take more action. This process creates an upward spiral, which means that the sky can truly be the limit.

Action Creates Results

> **Luke 11:10**
> *For everyone who asks, receives. Everyone who seeks, finds. And to everyone who knocks, the door will be opened.*

Let's consider the above words from Luke, in addition to the passage from Matthew that opened this chapter. An "open-door policy" of sorts is what makes the principle of action creates results work—you only have to walk through the door; take action, and you will have your results. You can decide not to walk through the door, and then you will fail your way through life. The door is always open. If you ask you will receive; if you don't ask you will not receive. No one can read your mind; you have to make your intensions known by asking.

If you seek you will find; if you don't seek you won't find. You cannot carry on by wishing for a better life without putting some effort into it. Get out there and start looking; start taking action; keep your mind open; start being more objective and less subjective and cynical. If you're not sure, ask—but when you ask, be sure to ask someone who has answers, someone you admire and seek to emulate, not your next-door neighbour. The rule of thumb is simple: **"Don't ask for advice from anyone who might be in the same situation you are trying to get out of; he or she is obviously unqualified to help you."** Instead, get expert advice from someone who has done it—or at least is getting the sort of results you're looking to achieve.

Knock and it shall be opened; don't knock and it won't be opened. You can't spend your entire life being afraid of what's behind the closed door! Granted, it can be scary venturing into the unknown; you might debate in your mind how other people will view you, or you might waste time thinking about how people will perceive you—will they think you have something meaningful to contribute, or will they laugh at you or judge you harshly? Well, I have found that most people are dealing with the same fears and trepidations, probably secretly wishing that you—or anyone—would do something first, so that they can come to terms with their own fears, telling themselves that if you can do it, maybe they can too. Remember this: life is not complicated at all; the worst of it is mostly imagined, thanks to our doubts and fears.

Chapter 9

THE PRINCIPLE

Diligence

> **Proverbs 22:29** (Amplified Bible)
> *Do you see a man diligent and skilful in his business?*
> *He will stand before kings; he will not stand before*
> *obscure men.*

I like the dictionary.com definition for **diligence** above all, which is "constant and earnest effort to accomplish what is undertaken; persistent exertion of body and mind". I prefer to describe diligence as **mastery** and **excellence,** qualities that are quite rare these days! People seem to have a haphazard approach to reaching their goals; it's as if they think that everything will just somehow fall into place and all will turn out fine.

I remember counselling a member of my team once, trying to help her see that there was a pattern to success which she was obviously missing, but she wasn't getting the point. I sought to help her understand that if she didn't change her attitude towards her business, she was likely to either quit or lose money. In other words, if she continued on the current path she would not succeed.

When nothing else seemed to work, I asked her to imagine that she could travel back in time and swap places with someone like Richard Branson early on in his career, before Virgin became what it is today. I told her, "Now imagine that you are running the earlier version of what's to become a multibillion dollar company, and you are running it with your current level of commitment to your present business.

Do you think there will be a Virgin PLC as we now know it today if its fate were in your hands then?"

Network marketing (or MLM) is a relatively simple business to build; however, the attitude that creates success in it is no different from that which is required in building a company like Virgin. The potential income in some network marketing companies can be in the six figures. I work with a company that has as much as £100,000 per month as its potential top income, and this can be achieved within five years if individuals take the right approach cultivate the right attitude. I'm talking about nothing less than excellence. Most people develop an attitude of mediocrity and resignation. They work to do a job, usually in a safe environment where they have no liabilities and few responsibilities, as whoever owns the company has to deal with those. If you just have a job, you can call in sick if you spent all night partying and wake up with a hangover.

My wife, Terri, is a manager at one of the top IT companies in the UK (actually, it's a multinational company). I can't even count how many times I have been woken up as early as six in the morning, because her mobile phone starts ringing, invariably with some staff member calling in with an excuse as to why he or she will not be able to work that day. Absurd things, such as, "My gerbil died, and I'm too emotional to come to work." I wonder what would happen if that person ran his or her own company and had a multimillion-dollar appointment on the same day that the gerbil died. I'm willing to bet that business owners in a similar situation would galvanise themselves to attend the appointment, but perhaps they wouldn't have allowed such a circumstance to put them in an emotional upheaval in the first place.

As I said, the work environment is a safe place; and for the sort of money most people make from a job, it's perfectly understandable that they don't seek to attain excellence. But in business—any business—the attitude has to be quite different, the commitment has to be above average, and the mastery of the particular skills required to be at the top of your game demands nothing less than excellence. In the business environment, the buck stops here—that is, the buck stops with you! It's not your co-worker's fault or your boss's fault; it's your fault. You, and only you, are responsible for all the results—whether successes or failures. That being the case, isn't it worth paying more attention to learning what it takes to succeed? Would it be a wise decision to change from the job mentality of "That's not my responsibility", or "I'm not being paid to do that", or "The company hasn't paid for my training yet" to a business mentality that decides, "Whatever it takes to win, I will do it; count me in—I'm ready to go, and I'm ready to do this!" That is the mentality that goes on to earn a six-figure income or that builds a Virgin PLC or a Microsoft.

The Bible verse quoted at the beginning of this chapter attests to the fact that diligence in your business affords you the privilege to stand before royalty and rub shoulders with dignitaries; you will not stand before obscure men. In long-standing British custom, the knighthood has been bestowed on hard-working, diligent men who have set themselves apart through sweat and guts, creating vast empires from scratch and often even without formal education. If you look around the world today—or if you study history—you will observe ordinary people achieving extraordinary things only because they have simply decided not to be average. Instead, they asked themselves, "What do I have to do to set me apart from the competition?" In order to answer that question, they dedicated time to discovering what that special ingredient was, and then they committed themselves to **mastering** the art and science of that field; they did their due diligence.

I remember a ten-year-old boy called Akai Osei; I think most people in this part of the world will remember him also. He was the winner of the 2010 *Got to Dance* championship. What many people are probably not aware of is the commitment and dedication that little boy had to put himself through in order to be crowned champion. Akai didn't need a lot of encouragement from his parents to be diligent; they actually thought he was working himself too hard. This child danced and practised at every opportunity. He went to school just like every other child, but he also attended dance classes regularly. He knew what he wanted and was prepared to do whatever it took to accomplish it. Remember, "There is nothing more powerful than a made-up mind"; something set him way above his peers. Quite simply, it was his diligence. Amazing that a ten-year-old child can understand diligence and excellence so well—principles that many adults are sometimes quite clueless about. The payout for winning this championship was £100,000.00—that is more than $160,000.00—above all, his fame has brought in movie contracts, TV shows, endorsements, and advertising contracts. He has met with celebrities and famous dignitaries; he has certainly stood before kings. *He will not stand before obscure men.*

The world is a stage, kind of like in the theatre. Imagine the entire stage is in darkness except for one single beam of light focused on stage; everything apart from the light is in darkness. Now the choice is clear for anyone who wants to achieve fame or fortune: you will have to step out of the darkness and into the spotlight. The attention is on you, and you will go places where those who refuse to step into the light will never go. Open the door, and all will be yours. Those who do not open the door or step into the light will have to spend the rest of their lives in obscurity, never realising their dreams or true potential.

Chapter 10

THE PRINCIPLE

Choice

> **Isaiah 1:19** (Amplified Bible)
> *If you are willing and obedient, you shall eat the good of the land.*

If is a conditional word that we can qualify into three categories:

1. **Conditional and Positive (If, and it is so):** this conditional **if** is based on an **absolute fact,** even though qualified by a conditional. An example of a conditional yet affirmative (positive) and factual would be, "If the sun rises tomorrow"; as this statement is true although qualified by the conditional **if.** (It is pretty much taken for granted that the sun will surely rise as it has done every day for billions of years.)

2. **Conditional but Negative (If, and it is not so):** this conditional **if** is based on an understanding that the statement could **never be true;** for example, "If only pigs could fly!" This conditional statement is based on an automatically impossible (negative) premise. (It might be nice if pigs could fly, but of course we know that will always be impossible and could never happen.)

3. **Conditional Yes and Conditional No (If, and it might be possible or it might not be):** This conditional **if** is somewhat more complicated; based on an absolute condition of choice and free will, the truth in this conditional statement is determined by the subject. It is so if the subject chooses to, or it is not so if the subject chooses not to. For example, "If you want to

you can get out of bed, stop feeling sorry for yourself, and go change your life around." The statement will be true only **if** the subject chooses to do it (conditional yes); it will be false if the subject chooses not to do it (conditional no).

Of all the creatures that inhabit our beautiful planet, humans are the only creatures that are truly self-determining. We are in our element when presented with challenges! We show a remarkable ability to face and overcome obstacles; more to the point, we do face and overcome them mostly by choice, often at the risk of terrible consequences and/or personal danger.

About 150 years ago in North America, thousands of ordinary people decided to head west to establish homesteads. They earned the name "pioneers"; these people packed up and headed west, into the unknown, fully aware that the journey would be hard and the consequences could be dire—many lost their scalps to the Native Americans determined to protect their lands and heritage.

In 1924 teacher and mountaineer George Mallory and his climbing partner, Andrew Irvine, embarked on the ill-fated expedition to ascend the summit of Mt Everest. In an interview before the expedition, when asked why he wanted to climb Everest, Mallory replied, "Because it's there."

On 12 September 1962, at Rice University in Houston, Texas, US President John F. Kennedy made an historic speech about his plan to put a man on the moon; here are some of his words from that famous speech: "We choose to go to the moon in this decade, not because it will be easy, but because it will be hard." Within ten years of that speech, people all over the planet watched Neil Armstrong and Buzz Aldrin walk on the moon—that event was definitely a gigantic leap for mankind.

The people who accomplished the things I described above did so just because they chose to. We each have the power to do what we need to do, but first we have to choose to do it! We have to decide to take a potential event or situation that could go either way—maybe it will happen or maybe it will not—but nevertheless we have to decide to muster all our willpower in order to make that potential event a reality. Sometimes it works out sometimes, and sometimes it doesn't; that's just part of life. But human beings must always try.

We enjoy many things today because those who came before us seized the moment to create, invent, or promote them. We even take many of these things for granted simply because they have been around for a while and so we have become disconnected from the history behind them. Great men faced ridicule and rejection from their peers in order to realise their own dreams. Such men chose to stand apart and face their critics, and history has proved they were right to take those risks. I'm referring to such people as John Logie Baird, inventor of television; Alexander Graham Bell, inventor of the telephone; Orville and Wilbur Wright, pilots of the first manned flight; and the list goes on.

How have humans been able to accomplish these things? Many ask the question, thinking the answer is complicated. It is not. The answer is simple: because we chose to.

Let's look at the third conditional **if** again. **If** God has given the human race one thing, it is the ability to decide how to write our history, both collective and personal history. The caveat is that history isn't written about nobodies; history only records greatness. The third conditional **if** puts the opportunity of becoming great into the hands of every living human being: maybe they each will do something with it, and maybe they each will not! That is the way it works; it is 100 per cent choice.

As the passage from Isaiah that opened this chapter advised, *If you are* (maybe you are maybe you are not) *willing and obedient you will eat the good of the land.* Immeasurable abundance and increase await any men or women who recognise the power within them, and who are willing to activate their choices, just as many before them have already done. You are not walking a path that is desolate and uncharted; success has always followed success! The rule of thumb has always been the same for those who participate in the journey towards success: If you can do it, so can I; follow the clues, study the past, make a choice, and I'll see you at the top.

The choice is yours, but you have to make it. What are you waiting for?

Recommended Books and Audio

Books

The Bible
Time for Success—Julio Melara
Parable of the Pipeline—Burke Hedges
Leaving a Legacy—Jim Paluch
Prosumer Power—Bill Quain
Think and Grow Rich—Napoleon Hill
Rich Dad Business School—Robert Kiyosaki
Seven Strategies for Wealth—Jim Rohn
Tough Times Never Last—Robert Schuller
The Choice—Og Mandino
Who Are You Really and What do You Want?—Shad Helstetter
Walking with the Wise—Linda Foresythe
Mind Games—Jeff Grout and Sarah Perrin
Grow Through It and Lead—Anthony & Jacqueline Thomas
Your Success Is Hidden in Your Daily Routine—Bernie De Souza
Live Your Dreams—Les Brown
The Secret—Rhonda Byrne

Audio/Video

The Strangest Secret—Earl Nightingale
Murphy's Committee—Jerry DRhino Clark
Changing Education Paradigms—Sir Ken Robinson (RSAnimate YouTube)

Lightning Source UK Ltd.
Milton Keynes UK
UKOW02f0014310814

237805UK00002B/100/P